W9-CXW-721

Foreword

Let's celebrate El Paso!

The book in your hands is a celebration of everything great about El Paso and the border region. It is the result of a monumental effort by people just like you. The photos inside tell a thousand stories about why we love it here, why we play here, and what makes El Paso like no other place on the planet.

"Capture El Paso" would not have been possible without the help of hundreds of photographers. Professionals and amateurs alike submitted thousands of images for this monumental book project. In all, hundreds of photographers submitted more than 9,000 photos, and the best rose to the top after we collected an astounding 727,919 votes. The rules for this one-of-a-kind project were simple: the photos with the most votes found their way into this book and into your hands.

The result is a book like none other.

Page after page, you will be surprised by what you find. With so many contributors from so many places, this book is possibly the most diverse and compelling representation of our great region. You will be transported from the rocky crags of Hueco Tanks to the glistening dunes of White Sands National Monument; from the waving maize fields of the Upper Valley to the splashy murals of Downtown El Paso. You will be introduced to residents young and old. Yet, just like in real life, the diversity of the area comes together in the following pages like a finely woven tapestry.

We are honored to present you with this record of who we are and where we are going, and we hope you take the time to read the stories behind the photos. Some were lucky happenstance; some took days for the right exposure. Some are of loved ones lost; some of strangers unknown. We only wish we could have included more photos in this book — that's why we included a DVD with hundreds of additional images. El Paso is truly too big for just one book.

Browse, read and, most of all, celebrate.

Ray M. Stafford
President and Publisher
El Paso Times

2

Table of Contents

About this book.

Capture El Paso 09™ is the most unique book project ever conceived. It started with a simple idea: Lots of folks take lots of pictures of the El Paso area — many of which would be worthy of publishing in a fine-art, coffee-table book. Knowing that thousands of photos would be submitted, the question was then posed: How do we pick the best from the rest?

The answer was genius. We put the editing power in the hands of the people. Local people. People that know El Paso. People just like you. We asked photographers, doctors, union workers, musicians, moms, right-handed people, pants-wearing folks, or anyone from any walk of life to vote for what they considered to be the photos that best capture the El Paso area.

From more than 9,000 photo submissions to the pages of this book, 727,919 votes helped shape what you hold in your hands. It's something that's never been done before: publishing by vote. Enjoy it.

How to use this book.

Open. Look at the best pictures you've ever seen. Repeat. Actually, maybe there's a little more to it. First, be sure to check out the prize winners in the back of the book (also marked with ★ throughout). You'll also want to watch the DVD. It's got more than a thousand photos on it! Here's the caption style so you can be sure to understand what's going on in each photo:

PHOTO TITLE *(position on page)*
Location photo taken, if available
Caption, mostly verbatim as submitted. ☞ **PHOTOGRAPHER**

Copyright info.

Copyright © 2009 • ISBN: 978-1-59725-225-6 | All rights reserved. No part of this book may be reproduced, stored in a retrieval system or transmitted in any form or by any means, electronic, mechanical, photocopying, recording or otherwise, without prior written permission of the copyright owner or the publisher. All photographers retain full rights of their photos that appear in this publication.

Do not use or copy any images from this book without written permission from the photographer. Note: photos may appear in different chapters than they were submitted. Prize awards were not affected. For more information on the Capture El Paso 09 Web site, please contact Pediment Publishing (books@pediment.com). Published by Pediment Publishing, a division of The Pediment Group, Inc. www.pediment.com. Printed in Canada. CAPTURE and Capture El Paso 09 are trademarks of The Pediment Group, Inc.

Friendly Faces

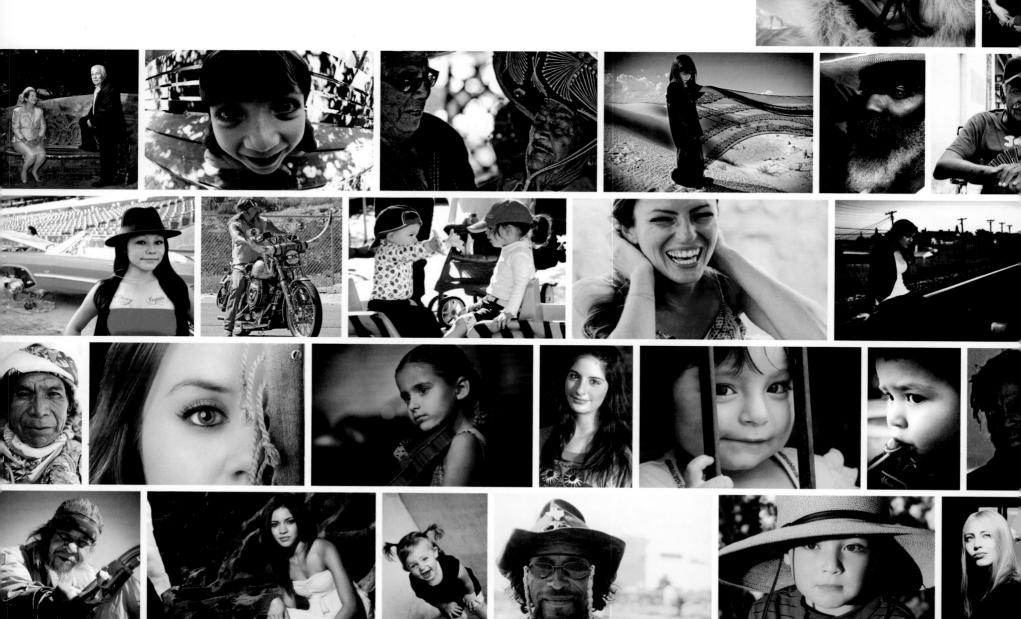

LITTLE SWIMMERS *(above)*
Enjoying a day at Elephant Butte.
LETICIA PENA

"My mom, at 70 years old, still walks over the bridge at least 3 times a week to buy stuff. She also gives to the poor who she calls her buddies. Maggie, pictured here, is her best buddy. At 80, she panhandles out of an abandoned doorway. She is proud that she doesn't beg, people "just happen" to give her money. She always wants to share her food with us and blesses us when we leave.
— **RICKY CARRASCO/MAGGIE**

TAVEN (above)
El Paso
Our grand nephew taking a nap. His mom stuck the cowboy hat on for the picture. 📷 **JEFFREY MCCLUER**

RUDOLFO GARCIA AND LA VIRGEN (left)
Mt. Cristo Rey
Rudolfo Garcia, deputy of Mt. Cristo Rey. 📷 **MELODY PARRA**

HOPPER (previous left)
Las Cruces, New Mexico
"Hopper," a blacksmith artisan from Hatch, poses during a session on street portraits. This gentle man with the great beard was enjoying a day at the Las Cruces Farmers Market. 📷 **BRENT CLARKE**

SADLY SMILING (previous middle)
Farmers Market
I was drawn by how sad this woman seemed while she feigned a smile for the camera. I spent the day at the Farmer's Market in Las Cruces taking street portraits. I love the honesty found in this environment.
📷 **BRENT CLARKE**

MAGGIE (previous right)
I took this at Ave. Juárez next to the Aduana post.
📷 **RICKY CARRASCO**

★ **HAMMOCKED** (following left)
El Paso
My beautiful baby boy enjoying himself in a hammock made by one of our many artisans here in El Paso, Texas. 📷 **MARVA FONSECA**

LYDIA LAUGHS (following right)
Hueco Tanks State Historic Site
When models crack up. Some of my favorite shots are that of spontaneous laughter. Here, Lydia laughs while on a photo shoot.
📷 **GEORGE PADILLA**

★ ERIKA MOLINA *(right)*
El Paso
My friend Erika getting ready for her amazing
career in modeling. 📷 **FERNIE CENICEROS**

UNTITLED *(opposite)*
Downtown
📷 **ELSA LOZADA**

TRADITION *(previous left)*
The pride of carrying on a musical tradition
is seen in the eyes of this young Mariachi.
📷 **BRENT CLARKE**

MIGHTY DUST *(previous right)*
Lower Valley, El Paso
Learning to live through the dust storms
that plague us during the spring.
📷 **MISS WATERTIGER**

I saw it... I looked for it...
Then I captured it.
— ELSA LOZADA/UNTITLED

FANTASTIC FRIENDS *(above)*
El Paso
Everyday should be full of surprises
and costumes!! It's great to be this age.
📷 **ERIKA JACKSON**

YOU CAN'T SEE ME! *(left)*
Little boy peeking — thinking he was hiding
from me. 📷 **LIRA DION**

**ALL-AMERICAN
CAT-EYED GIRL** *(far left)*
El Paso
Nothing says summer like swimming-pool
time! 📷 **SANDRA BALBOA**

Arts, Culture & Food

STRANGER IN A STRANGE LAND *(above)*
Hatch, New Mexico
The Hatch Chile Festival has some beautiful chile to offer. Love the colors and the way they stood out against the larger red chiles.
📷 **EFRAIN MENDOZA**

★ **MAZATZIN** *(following left)*
Juárez Plaza
A few months ago, my mom invited me to photograph some of the street people she has made friends with on the main strip and the Mercado in Juárez. We found Mazatzin in traditional Aztec garb dancing in front of the Cathedral. When he saw me shooting, he got into the classic archer pose. 📷 **RICKY CARRASCO**

META ART *(following middle top)*
EPCC Valle Verde
The charcoal drawing of an EPCC art student seems to bring out the black and white tones in the room. 📷 **NEIL DAVIS**

THE FEEL *(following middle bottom)*
Friend's house in the Upper Valley
Whatever a person decides to create from clay, they must fully feel the subject or it will not turn out. 📷 **JOHN GLOVER**

A NEW HOPE AT THE PLAZA *(following right top)*
The Plaza
Great night to watch a movie. 📷 **RICARDO CARRILLO**

CLAY WITH FORM *(following right bottom)*
El Paso
Stacked clay pots bake in the afternoon sun. The unique pottery which is familiar to the border is sought by folks all over the U.S.
📷 **BRENT CLARKE**

AGUAS FRESCAS (above)
Rancho Market, Ysleta
Delicious aguas frescas are heaven sent on hot El Paso summer days.
📷 HELEN BREWER

HANDS (top left)
El Paso
The hands of a hard working lady preparing Pico de Gallo, a spicy sauce popular in Mexican cuisine. 📷 ENRIQUE VILLAR

A LITTLE OF BOTH (bottom left)
La Union, New Mexico
She was baggin' up a bag with yellow and purple onions.
📷 DENNIS QUINTANA

GRAPES FROM MY YARD (opposite)
El Paso
Every summer we enjoy these lovely grapes that are grown in our backyard. 📷 LAURA NATIVIDAD

RIFF RAFF ATTACK (following left)
No Man's Land (Lower Valley)
Cody one-ups the punx. 📷 CESAR PEREZ II

BAR-MITZVAH PRACTICE (following right)
Temple Mt. Sinai, El Paso
My little brother reading from the Torah as practice for his Bar-Mitzvah at Temple Mt. Sinai. 📷 EITHAN KOTKOWSKI

23

LA DIVINA *(above)*
Downtown El Paso
An artist finishes his creation at the event "Chalk the Block." 📷 **BIANCA BOURGEOIS**

WISE LATINO *(right)*
Lincoln Park
Artist/Educator Gabriel Gaytan is currently working on a mural titled "Corazon de El Paso" (not pictured) in Lincoln Park.
📷 **RICKY CARRASCO**

TEXAS HYPERSPACE *(far right)*
UTEP Library
Or The Texas Wedge, the sculpture in front of the UTEP Library by James Macbeth, at night.
📷 **RICKY CARRASCO**

LIQUIDSKIN *(above)*
Alfresco Fridays, Downtown El Paso
Lead singer of "Liquid Skin" displays her style.
📷 **MISS WATERTIGER**

THE MC *(opposite left)*
Las Cruces, New Mexico
This colorful character with his real green chile bow tie and megaphone, enjoys a break with a snow cone. Soon it will be back to his duties as part MC, Comedian, Administrator and all-around good guy at the Las Cruces Farmers Market. 📷 **BRENT CLARKE**

DAYS OF TEQUILA AND LOVELY SENORITAS *(opposite right)*
Las Cruces, New Mexico
An old man strums what looks like an even older guitar, and sings of his youth and lost loves.
📷 **BRENT CLARKE**

WHICH TEQUILA ARE YOU? *(following top left)*
El Paso
Everyone has their favorite! 📷 **LAURA NATIVIDAD**

SALT SHAKERS *(following bottom left)*
Las Cruces
A vendor's table at the Farmers Market in Las Cruces. 📷 **JEFFREY MCCLUER**

SPLASH OF LIME *(following bottom middle)*
El Paso
Everything tastes better with a little splash of lime. 📷 **G. LEWIS SMITH**

STILL BEFORE THE STORM *(following top middle)*
Camino Real Hotel-Dome Bar
The golden hour before the cocktail hour.
📷 **MISS WATERTIGER**

SEA OF GREEN *(following top right)*
El Paso
The shots of green sauce at Chico's Tacos. I had to fight back an angry mob of green sauce fanatics so I could get this shot. 📷 **CHAD BEATY**

UNTITLED *(following bottom right)*
Watch out, those chiles will get you!
📷 **JOSH LUTTRELL**

TINY DANCERS *(above)*
East El Paso
📷 **SANDRA BALBOA**

DEATH *(left)*
Mesilla, New Mexico
Captured inside the Galeria located in Old
Mesilla in celebration of "Día de los Muertos."
📷 **MARVA FONSECA**

**HORSESHOES AND
SKULLS** *(opposite)*
Decorations. 📷 **BIANCA BOURGEOIS**

"The border's Texican culture is alive and well in El Paso.— **SANDRA BALBOA/TINY DANCERS**

VIOLINS UNDER THE SKY (above)
Chamizal
Members of the El Paso Symphony Orchestra playing at the 4th of July celebration at Music under the Stars. 📷 **RICKY CARRASCO**

FORGIVE THEM FATHER... (left)
Outskirts of El Paso
Stark grapevines, supported by wire, rests in the dusty fields of morning at the winery on Highway 28. 📷 **MISS WATERTIGER**

CONQUISTADOR (opposite)
El Paso
Representation of the first thanksgiving.
📷 **ERIKA JACKSON**

★ **FOLKLORICO**
DANCER (following left)
Central old Mesilla. 📷 **CESAR PEREZ II**

SURRENDER (following right)
San Elizario
Actors perform the reenactment of the first Thanksgiving with The El Paso Mission Trail.
📷 **EFRAIN MENDOZA**

Pets

STEWART *(left)*
📷 **LAURA NATIVIDAD**

★ **LUCCA TRESPALACIOS** *(following left)*
Dulce Tierra Drive
This is our beloved pug! His name is Lucca and I love the way he looks at me. By the way, he is looking for a girlfriend!!!
📷 **MARTHA PAOLA TRESPALACIOS**

UNTITLED *(following top)*
Pj and Holly. 📷 **JOSH LUTTRELL**

10 YEAR BUD *(following bottom)*
El Paso
My best pal for 10 years and counting — he was a stray on the west side. He's a retired police dog. We have traveled the world together. His nose is raw from burying a huge ham bone my neighbor threw over the fence. Doesn't matter what comes over my fence though, he WILL bury it. 📷 **MISS WATERTIGER**

" The little scratch on his nose was done by a cat that got into the yard. He beat up Stewart and scratched him all up, but he recovered quite well. Stewart is a big rabbit so I know he gave the cat a good fight.
— **LAURA NATIVIDAD/STEWART**

THE GREETER *(right)*
Fabens
This friendly horse greets customers as they
come and go at the Cattleman's Steakhouse.
📷 **GEORGE PADILLA**

EVENING FEEDING *(far right)*
Upper Valley
Having their evening snack. 📷 **DENNIS QUINTANA**

'UGH, SNOW *(opposite)*
Socorro
My baby donkey in the snow on a brisk winter
morning. 📷 **HELEN BREWER**

WHO LOVES YOU??? *(top)*
El Paso
And the winner is... 📷 **AVI KOTKOWSKI**

NICOLAS *(bottom)*
El Paso
Just having fun!! 📷 **AVI KOTKOWSKI**

BIG EAR *(far left)*
El Paso
Our dog Hope loves to lay her head against the
outside brick with this kind of pose. Go figure.
📷 **BRENT CLARKE**

★ **THE WHINY WEIMY** *(following left)*
Central El Paso
Our new Weimaraner puppy, Jacob.
📷 **NASTASSIA ARTALEJO**

THE COOLEST... *(following right)*
El Paso
Cat...and he knows it. 📷 **MISS WATERTIGER**

CONSPIRACY (above)
El Paso
Conspiracy: They are discussing ringing the door bell and then running — little pranksters.
📷 MISS WATERTIGER

BITE OUT OF CRIME... (right)
El Paso
...But not the water bill. My dog loves to chase the water (and the lawn mower), but I noticed the older he gets, the closer he gets to my hand. Guess he's conserving energy. 📷 MISS WATERTIGER

ZINNA (opposite)
Far West Texas
Zinna: The Trail Warrior Dog. According to her owner she is a very old dog. I only saw a lively pup who fearlessly led the way. She guards the ancient drawings behind her. 📷 MISS WATERTIGER

WHERE'S MY HAY? *(left)*
Canutillo
📷 **SHANNON HIATT**

FIERCE *(opposite top left)*
El Paso
The stare of want. 📷 **RUTH ESTRADA**

SKY DOG *(opposite bottom left)*
Resting inside on a warm summer's day.
📷 **BIANCA BOURGEOIS**

THE NEIGHBOR'S CAT *(opposite top right)*
El Paso
Personally, I'm not a big fan of cats, however
there is something about this particular cat
that I really like. He always seems to be posing
for cameras. 📷 **EITHAN KOTKOWSKI**

IT'S A BIG WORLD OUT THERE!
(opposite bottom right)
White Sands, New Mexico
Our miniature Yorkie, Rusty, seems even small-
er in the endless dunes. 📷 **LAURA NATIVIDAD**

❝ Not sure if a goat is a
pet or not if its job is to keep
the weeds down, but "Hotdog"
sure is inquisitive.
— **SHANNON HIATT/WHERE'S MY HAY?**

Scapes of All Sorts

HUECO TANKS (above)
El Paso
Some of the Mountains at Hueco Tanks
National Park. 📷 **CARLOS VALDEZ**

END OF DAYS (following left)
Anthony Gap, New Mexico
The last colors of the day serve as a backdrop
to a windmill on the old Mussman ranch.
📷 **BRENT CLARKE**

RED SKY AT NIGHT (following right)
Anthony Gap, New Mexico
Star trails fill the sky as a windmill remains
motionless on the old Mussman ranch.
📷 **BRENT CLARKE**

ASCARATE LAKE *(above)*
El Paso
Yup, that's water here in the desert city of El Paso. You can fish, you can boat and jet ski, but as for swimming, leave that to the pros: the ducks. 📷 **ELIAS REVELES**

YELLOWS AND BLUES *(left)*
Chaparral, New Mexico
A strange cloud formation fills the sky, while a sea of yellow poppies crowd the ground below.
📷 **BRENT CLARKE**

DESERT SOUTHWEST *(opposite)*
Near Fabens
One of the many old weathered fences found in the desert southwest. 📷 **ALONZO RIVERA**

COTTON FIELD *(above)*
El Paso
A cotton field at sunset between El Paso and
Mesilla on highway 28. 📷 **JEFFREY MCCLUER**

TAKE OFF *(right)*
Bosque del Apache Wetlands
Thousands of northern migrates take to the
sky looking for their early morning breakfast.
📷 **BRENT CLARKE**

LAST LIGHT *(following left)*
New Mexico
A break of light illuminates the dunes just
before sunset at White Sands National Monument. 📷 **BRENT CLARKE**

THE ROCK *(following right)*
Hueco Tanks National Park, just outside of El
Paso. Taken in December 2008. 📷 **D BOWDEN**

WYLER TRAMWAY *(left)*
El Paso
Tower at the top of the Wyler Tramway.
📷 **JEFFREY MCCLUER**

BEAUTY IN BLUE *(right)*
The reflection of the sky on the windows gives
it a touch of beauty. 📷 **M SYLVIA FABELA**

WINDMILL, MOON, AND STARS *(above)*
El Paso
Windmill near Anthony Gap. 📷 **JEFFREY MCCLUER**

FADING LIGHT *(following top)*
Central El Paso
Panoramic picture. 📷 **ENRIQUE VILLAR**

CHRISTMAS LIGHTS AT SAN JACINTO PLAZA
(following bottom)
Downtown El Paso
San Jacinto Plaza is the heart of El Paso and is fully decorated for
Christmas by the Parks and Recreation Department. 📷 **AL BRADEN**

DOWNTOWN EL PASO AT DUSK
(following right)
Shot from Scenic Drive. 📷 **RAY CHIARELLO**

PRIVATE PARADISE *(left)*
Curbside oasis.
📷 **CHITO B**

SUNSET OVER EL PASO STREET
(far left)
El Paso
Photograph taken in downtown.
📷 **ENRIQUE VILLAR**

LAVENDER *(below)*
Upper Valley
So tiny and beautiful!!!
📷 **MARTHA PAOLA TRESPALACIOS**

FULL MOON AT THE FRANKLIN'S
(above)
El Paso
The beauty of the full moon over Franklin
Mountain. 📷 **AVI KOTKOWSKI**

URBAN CHAOS *(left)*
El Paso
A very, very old and rusting fire escape
graphs itself into a building downtown.
📷 **BRENT CLARKE**

GREAT ASPIRATIONS *(opposite)*
Near Anthony
Little seedlings are only beginning to sprout as
12-foot maze stocks in the background show
off their great stature, in a farm field in the
Upper Valley. 📷 **BRENT CLARKE**

69

BARBED... *(above)*
El Paso
...And wire. 📷 **MISS WATERTIGER**

TIGER SWALLOWTAIL *(left)*
Westside El Paso
A frequent visitor to my yard. 📷 **RAY CHIARELLO**

BEE & THISTLE *(opposite)*
El Paso
A healthy sized bumble bee eagerly collects pollen from this unusual, thistle-like plant near Union Station. 📷 **KERRIGAN SWAN-GARCIA**

GOLDEN VALLEY *(following left)*
Near La Union, New Mexico
Just before nightfall, the sun throws the day's last light on a recent harvested cotton field and cottonwood trees. 📷 **BRENT CLARKE**

SUNSET AT HIDEAWAY LAKE
(following right)
Outside El Paso
📷 **LIRA DION**

71

"I really felt like this image captured a beauty unseen by the naked eye. — **LIRA DION/SUNSET AT HIDEAWAY LAKE**

MOONRISE OVER EAST EL PASO
(above)
Mt. Franklin
Moonrise over East El Paso from Wyler Tram
State Park. 📷 **AL BRADEN**

LUNAR VIEW FROM ZION *(right)*
Northeast Mountain Park, El Paso
Lunar View from Zion, taken with a Celestron
C6, 6-inch refractor at 1200 mm focus.
📷 **JOHN COLLINS**

VIEW INTO MY WORLD *(far right)*
El Paso
Long exposure night photography at scenic
drive. 📷 **TOM GAGE**

TEXAS CONDO *(top)*
New Mexico
At first glance, I thought she was a plastic owl until I saw her head move and eyes followed me as I walked across the field near White Sands Missile Range. She had a huge baby beneath her! She told me the tenants above moved out and broke their lease.
📷 **MISS WATERTIGER**

OWL EYE *(bottom)*
This unfortunate horned owl was scheduled for humane euthanasia at Crossroads Animal Hospital El Paso/Chihuanuan Desert Wildlife Rescue. His extensive and irreparable injuries were due to hitting an electric wire, then an automobile. His head was still magnificent and I wanted to capture his essence in life prior to his transition over to death. Very sad situation indeed, but he lives on in this photo.
📷 **MARK LENOX**

LITTLE INJURED BIRD *(opposite top left)*
I came upon this bird, and for whatever reason he wouldn't move. I was thinking he was injured but when I came back, he was gone.
📷 **LIRA DION**

★ **STROLLING** *(opposite bottom left)*
Keystone Heritage Park, El Paso
Strolling at Keystone Park. 📷 **AVI KOTKOWSKI**

GOLDEN FLIGHT *(opposite top right)*
Bosque del Apache Wetlands
Canadian Snow Geese enjoy the flight and warmer temps found in southern New Mexico.
📷 **BRENT CLARKE**

MALE RUFOUS HUMMINGBIRD
(opposite bottom right)
Westside El Paso
During the spring, these birds migrate up the Pacific coast from the interior of Mexico all the way up to southern Alaska. By mid-summer, they make their return trip south along the eastern portion of the Rocky Mountains, which takes them through El Paso during July and August. 📷 **RAY CHIARELLO**

RISE AND SHINE *(above)*
Rim Road
El Paso sunrise. 📷 **DIANE SIERRA**

★ **MT. CRISTO REY** *(top left)*
El Paso
Sunset at Mt. Cristo Rey. 📷 **RAY NAVARRO**

FIREBIRD *(bottom left)*
El Paso
This shot was taken at sunset on June 23rd, 2008 after some west El Paso monsoon action. This is one of a spectacular series of frames watching this beautiful sunset unfold. 📷 **TIM O'MALLEY**

★ **HERE COMES THE SUN** *(opposite)*
New Mexico
The beauty of living in El Paso is that it is surrounded by so many great places easy and quick to visit. This early morning photo was taken at the Bosque Del Apache National Wildlife Refuge. 📷 **GEORGE PADILLA**

TANA WALKS *(top)*
El Paso
Tana walks down one of the many dirt roads
that divide farm lands along the Rio Grande
Valley. 📷 **GEORGE PADILLA**

COLLECTION *(bottom)*
📷 **ANGELINE STEWART**

**THE TREE OF
ETERNAL REST**
(far right)
The Cemetery at La Isla, Fabens
An old tree that no longer lives joins those
who have been laid to rest at the cemetery.
📷 **BRENT CLARKE**

"Thanksgiving Day: The
aunts are hard at work in the
kitchen, and I'm wandering
around Grandma's eclectic
garden, bird-watching. I drag
my skirt through the grass,
and get it wet; my toes are
cold. I can see my breath. The
house is bubbling with activ-
ity, but the garden is quiet. It's
the only time that day that I
will be alone.
— ANGELINE STEWART/COLLECTION

SPRING *(above)*
Lower Valley, El Paso
In full bloom. 📷 **MISS WATERTIGER**

PRIOR PURPLE *(top)*
El Paso
Now I think it's blue. 📷 **MISS WATERTIGER**

SOLID AS A ROCK *(left)*
El Paso
Solid as a Rock — that is, just about everything in El Paso! 📷 **MISS WATERTIGER**

CHIVES FLOWERS *(far left)*
The Upper Valley
My best friend Zonia has one of the most beautiful gardens I've ever seen. I took this photo while pet-sitting for her Chihuahuas Carmelo and Silverio.
📷 **MARTHA PAOLA TRESPALACIOS**

AUTUMN (top)
Upper Valley, El Paso
Beautiful Autumn day. 📷 **RENEE IGLESIAS**

THE CHANGING OF THE COLORS
(bottom)
Guadalupe Mountains
📷 **RUDY HERNANDEZ**

CRISTO REY (far right)
Westside
A precious symbol in El Paso.
📷 **BERTHA BOURGEOIS**

"This is another one of El Paso's great local icons — the Guadalupe Mountains. Every year people from all over Texas come to witness this spectacular event that happens around late October to early November — the changing of the color of the leaves. These bright colors displayed are very impressive.
— **RUDY HERNANDEZ/THE CHANGING OF THE COLORS**

THUNDERSTORM *(above)*
Downtown El Paso
Picture taken in South El Paso.
📷 **ENRIQUE VILLAR**

MOTHER NATURE VISITING WEST TEXAS *(opposite)*
East of El Paso
Chasing Monsoons. 📷 **TRAVIS BERRYMAN**

" Everyone has a stomping ground when they were a kid. This was mine. The desert of El Paso out by Hueco Tanks. My friends and I would drive 32 miles to get here and climb rocks, explore caves and basically enjoy nature all day. The desert isn't for everyone. Some feel it to be sparse and dead. I personally find it beautiful. You can breath out here. There is space. The view of the sky (Cielo Vista) is amazing at times. I took this shot when I went home for Christmas of 2008. I need to go home more often. — **D BOWDEN/HOME IS WHERE YOUR HEART IS**

HOME IS WHERE YOUR HEART IS *(left)*
El Paso
◙ **D BOWDEN**

YUCK-A *(opposite)*
El Paso
Somewhere in the desert of East El Paso.
◙ **D BOWDEN**

Newsworthy

THE COMMUNITY (top)
East El Paso
Local El Pasoans get ready to build the Ruiz family a new home on "Extreme Makeover: Home Edition." 📷 **WILLIAM DUNN**

STAND PROUD (bottom)
Extreme Home Makeover and the El Paso community helped complete a new home for Maria Ruiz and her family January 2009.
📷 **XOCHITL BUDDÈ**

CUB SCOUT *(above)*
Fort Bliss
Cub scout placing flags on Memorial Day.
📷 **MARVIN HANLEY**

**A VAQUERO'S
FINAL RIDE** *(left)*
Fabens
Hats and rope tell the story of a local vaquero
who rests at La Isla cemetery. 📷 **GEORGE PADILLA**

★ **FIRE IN JUÁREZ.** *(opposite top)*
El Paso
Wildfire in Juárez could be seen anywhere
in El Paso. The smoke filled the skies for
two whole days! Taken at sunset on my roof.
📷 **CARLOS VALDEZ**

DRUG BUST *(opposite bottom)*
East El Paso
A police canine with 154 pounds of
marijuana that he located hidden in furniture.
📷 **AARON CURLEE**

BORDER FENCE (above)
Border with Mexico and USA
The border fence...controversy.
📷 **AVI KOTKOWSKI**

GIDDY UP! (left)
Transmountain Road
This sculpture greets visitors to the Border
Patrol museum in Northeast El Paso. This shot
was spotted by my mom on one of my shooting trips. I have enjoyed Capture because I've
had the opportunity to show Mom many parts
of El Paso she's never known even existed and
given us lots of quality time. 📷 **RICKY CARRASCO**

★ **ENGULFED** (far left)
Ascarate Park, El Paso
El Paso Fire Training Academy. Live Fire
Training for the EPCC Cadets. EPCC
Trainee, Jake Canavan and Chief Dave Conklin
(White Helmet) take on the fury of flames.
📷 **GEORGE TAUSIANI**

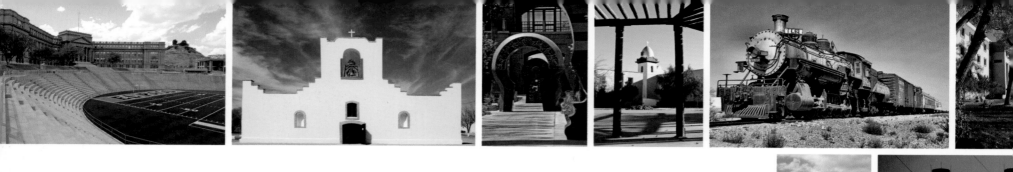

Schools & Institutions

EQUESTRIAN STATUE *(top)*
Airway Boulevard
Equestrian sculpture at El Paso Airport.
📷 **AL BRADEN**

COMING TOGETHER *(bottom)*
Roswell
Many volunteers coming together to build a
Kingdom Hall. 📷 **RUTH ESTRADA**

SORORRO MISSION *(following top)*
Socorro
Socorro Mission. 📷 **AL BRADEN**

SNOW-CAPPED HEAD STONES
(following bottom)
Fort Bliss Cemetery
Snow powdered the headstones, 2007.
📷 **APRIL EL PASO PORTRAITS**

THE CHURCH AT LA ISLA
(following right)
Near Fabens
An old church stands by itself amongst the cotton fields of the Lower Valley. 📷 **BRENT CLARKE**

RUSHING *(left)*
Downtown El Paso
Man with sunbrella rushes past the fountain
during his lunch break. 📷 **MISS WATERTIGER**

FINGERS OF GOD
TOUCHING THE DEAD *(right)*
La Isla
Was on a family picnic in the area. We stopped
to have lunch at the church nearby. The thun-
derstorms were starting to build. I waited until
the rays of the sun were at their highest and
took the photo. 📷 **TRAVIS BERRYMAN**

WALKING TOWARDS THE LIGHT
(opposite left)
El Paso
A shot from inside the San Ysleta Mission,
a place of vast history, hope, and holiness.
📷 **KERRIGAN SWAN-GARCIA**

OUR PROTECTOR *(opposite top)*
Las Cruces
Virgin Mary outside Mesilla church.
📷 **GERARDO GARIBAY**

SMELTER CEMETERY *(opposite bottom)*
Smeltertown
📷 **KERRIGAN SWAN-GARCIA**

"Just shy of the shadows cast by Mt. Cristo Rey exists a field of sacred ground, the story of an enduring community, and the complex past of Smeltertown. Over 125 years of El Paso history lie here in Smelter Cemetery and tributes of every kind attest to the strength and devotion of the people who built it.
— KERRIGAN SWAN-GARCIA/SMELTER CEMETERY

WELCOME TO THE CORTEZ (above)
Downtown
Beautiful work welcomes you to The Cortez.
📷 **M SYLVIA FABELA**

HISTORIC UNION STATION (top left)
El Paso
The lobby of the historic Union Station is
one of El Paso's finest works of classic
architecture, a place where one can hear the
history of the city echoing from wall to wall.
📷 **KERRIGAN SWAN-GARCIA**

COLOR AND CHROME (bottom left)
War Eagles Air Museum, New Mexico
There are more than just planes to view at the
Air Museum. 📷 **CHAD BEATY**

MOTEL, HOTEL (opposite)
El Paso
But not Holiday Inn. 📷 **MISS WATERTIGER**

CROSS FIRE *(above)*
St. Pius X Church, El Paso
Sometimes we get caught in the cross fire, but whenever I look up, I always feel much better.
📷 **MISS WATERTIGER**

**GOLDEN MAZE AT
THE PLAZA** *(right)*
Downtown El Paso
A golden maze fills the awning at The Plaza Theatre downtown. 📷 **BRENT CLARKE**

★ **A CANDLE AMONG THEM** *(far right)*
St. Pius Church
📷 **SHARO DICKERSON**

SONORA RESTAURANT *(previous left)*
Lower Valley
Main entrance to the Sonora Restaurant.
📷 **FERNIE ESCOBAR**

SAN ELI LIGHT *(previous right)*
San Elizario
An early morning sunrise along with a light rain, paints the sky and cleans the old chapel down. 📷 **BRENT CLARKE**

★ **THE OLD THEATER** *(following left)*
Downtown El Paso
The Plaza Theatre. 📷 **MARVIN HANLEY**

THE PLAZA THEATRE *(following right)*
Downtown El Paso
The Plaza Theatre. 📷 **ENRIQUE VILLAR**

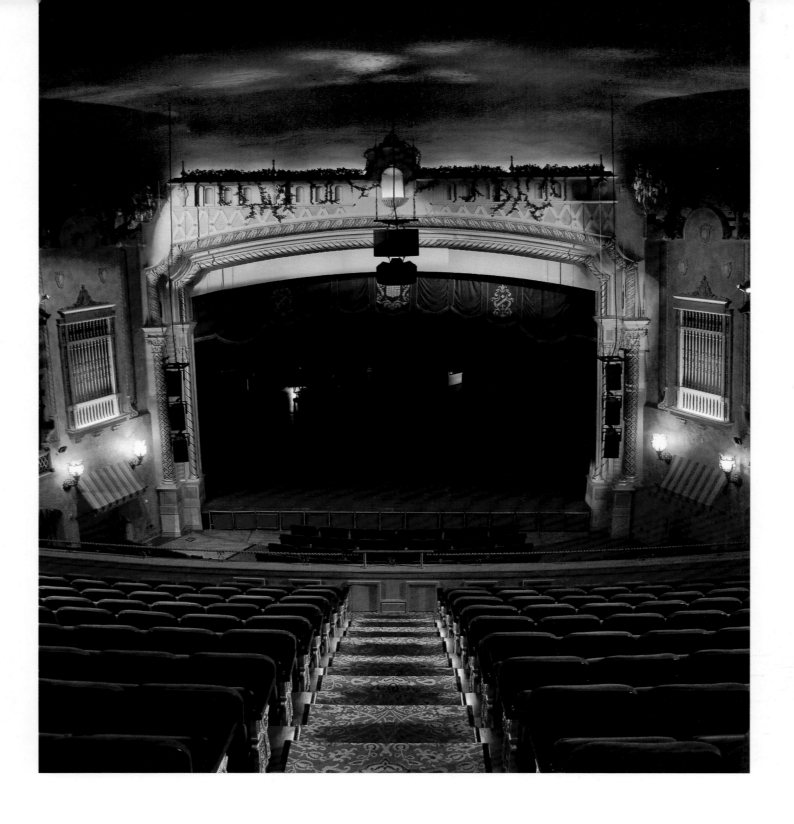

" One of the beautiful features and structures in St. Pius Church is this big fountain that is found in the center of the plaza. The sky was filled with feathery clouds, the air smelled of fresh grass, and the sun was smiling graciously upon the area when I was visiting to take pictures.
— SHARO DICKERSON/QUENCH MY THIRST

PANORAMIC PHOTOGRAPHY *(above)*
El Paso
I wanted to show how UTEP looks when the sunset hits it just right.
📷 JACQUELINE FLYNN

EL PASO HIGH SCHOOL *(left)*
El Paso
Photograph of El Paso High. 📷 ENRIQUE VILLAR

PILL BOXES AND REFLECTIONS *(opposite top)*
El Paso
The county building reflects the Federal Courthouse downtown, with the pill box barriers in the foreground. 📷 BRENT CLARKE

CANDLES BURN AT YSLETA MISSION *(opposite bottom)*
El Paso
The shared histories of native Pueblo Indians, Spanish explorers, and Franciscan missionaries converge here at Ysleta Mission, officially established in 1680. Both external and internal design elements refer to this interaction of cultures and give modern day visitors a rare glance into the long, rich heritage of the people of El Paso.
📷 KERRIGAN SWAN-GARCIA

QUENCH MY THIRST *(opposite right)*
St. Pius Church
📷 SHARO DICKERSON

Everyday Life

UNTITLED *(previous)*
Fox Plaza, El Paso
An old man dyes a young man's boots. 📷 **MELODY PARRA**

FROGFEST EL PASO ZOO 2008 *(left)*
A little girl looks at a bullfrog at Frogfest 2008 at the El Paso Zoo.
📷 **ARMANDO VELA**

IN THE GARDEN *(right)*
My mother and grandmother taking a stroll.
📷 **ANGELINE STEWART**

★ **ME TOO!!!** *(above)*
West El Paso
Mom's present in Mother's Day!
📷 **GERARDO GARIBAY**

PEOPLE IN EVERY DIRECTION...
(above)
Raynolds Overpass at midnight.
📷 **RICKY CARRASCO**

NO NEED TO CHANGE A THING...
(right)
Juárez
Jose Carmen has been making boots by hand in Juárez for more than 20 years. I found him working at this little shop behind the strip. Although the hype has centered on the bloodbath, simple hardworking men like Mr. Carmen are the backbone of Juárez. 📷 **RICKY CARRASCO**

UNTITLED *(opposite top)*
White Sands
The dunes continue to evoke a variety of creative and positive experiences that only one can fully understand. 📷 **SHARO DICKERSON**

FUTURE FIREFIGHTERS *(opposite bottom)*
EPCC Valle Verde
Mayra Orozco, a first year Fire Techie, learning to chop through a roof. If you're planning to have an emergency in about 3 years, expect Mayra and her crew to be ready. When I taught a Fire Tech class in high school a few years ago, the underclassmen (boys) would ask if girls could be firefighters. All I would have to do is motion to Moni or Lety to answer the question.
📷 **RICKY CARRASCO**

JUST GOT HITCHED *(opposite right)*
El Paso Botanical Gardens
The day was beautiful, serene, and very festive! An array of burnt orange and sunshine yellow filled the sky as this couple said their vows in front of family, friends, and special guests. 📷 **SHARO DICKERSON**

SUMMER IN THE CITY *(above)*
El Paso
At the swimming pool. 📷 **JERZY MOLON**

OLD MEMORIES *(right)*
San Jose Road
A Sunday afternoon drive. 📷 **MIRANDA ROSS**

★ **MINI ME** *(far right)*
"I want to be just like my Daddy." I thought these two were so cute in
their matching shoes. 📷 **LIRA DION**

TRES AMIGOS *(above)*
El Paso
Just another day in downtown.
📷 **ERIKA JACKSON**

ALL AMERICAN MUSCLE *(opposite)*
Barnett Harley-Davidson
SFC Ostheimer (Iowa) and SSG Dewitt (N.
Carolina), both currently stationed at Ft.
Bliss, try on a couple of Harley V-Rods.
📷 **RICKY CARRASCO**

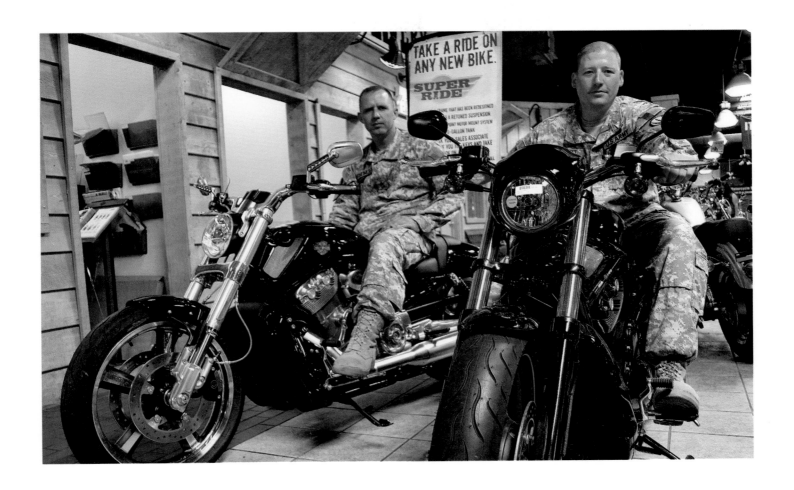

“Soldiers like this are the reason El Paso continues to prosper and the rest of us can ride hard and ride free! Thanks guys!
— RICKY CARRASCO/ALL AMERICAN MUSCLE

Sports & Recreation

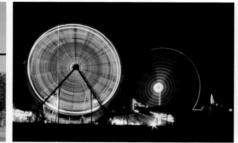

TEQUILA BAR *(above)*
One of my best friends, Andrew J. Espinosa,
shooting pool at the Garage/Tequila Bar.
📷 **MARVA FONSECA**

SUPER MARISELA *(following top)*
El Paso Country Club
A true champion! 📷 **GERARDO GARIBAY**

COLOR IN THE DESERT *(following bottom)*
White Sands
White Sands Balloon Fest, 2009. 📷 **RENEE IGLESIAS**

★ **TRAINING** *(following right)*
White Sands
Dorota Gruca, professional marathon
runner, after her training on White Sands.
📷 **JERZY MOLON**

**INDEPENDENCE DAY
(FOURTH OF JULY)** (above)
U.S.-Mexico Border
📷 **FERMIN ROBLEDO**

THE BATTLE OF I-10 (top left)
Our epic rivalry: UTEP vs NMSU.
📷 **VALERIE FACIO**

MUSIC UNDER THE STARS (bottom left)
Chamizal National Memorial
Fourth of July concert goers. 📷 **RAY CHIARELLO**

"A great fireworks show, every kid's and photographer's dream! — **FERMIN ROBLEDO/
INDEPENDENCE DAY (FOURTH OF JULY)**

127

"I really love to watch these young kids in person. I'm always impressed with the things they manage to do on a little skateboard.
— FERMIN ROBLEDO/SKYBOARDING

WAIT FOR THE CUE (top left)
Downtown El Paso
A four year old boy waits for his cue to skate in front of a large crowd during the second annual Chalk the Block event. 📷 **CEASAR TORRES**

SKYBOARDING (bottom left)
Parque Extremo, Cd Juárez
📷 **FERMIN ROBLEDO**

UNTITLED (opposite)
Bill Luttrell has some fun out in the desert. 📷 **JOSH LUTTRELL**

RIO GRANDE JUMP (below)
El Paso/Juárez
Eddie Wearden jumps the Rio Grande. 📷 **ED CORDOVA**

A FLOWER LIKE NO OTHER *(above)*
Western Playland, El Paso
Resembling a giant flower, this ride is waiting
for children and adults alike to laugh and
scream with glee. 📷 **CHAD BEATY**

★ **A MORNING FLIGHT** *(right)*
Anthony Gap
A balloon coasts over the foothills of the
Franklin Mountains during the annual Balloon
Festival. 📷 **BRENT CLARKE**

THAT'S MY HORSE! *(above)*
El Paso Rodeo
Wow what a ride! 📷 **TONI MARIE**

NECK TO NECK *(left)*
SAC El Paso
📷 **CARLOS VALDEZ**

RACING *(opposite)*
Sunland Park
Horse racing at Sunland Park Racetrack.
📷 **TIM SYBRANT**

"It was a close call, but Montwood took the race at the district track meet held at the SAC. Was able to use my uncle's 300mm f/2.8 lens for a couple of shots!!! It's an amazing piece of glass. — **CARLOS VALDEZ/NECK TO NECK**

EYE TO EYE. *(above)*
The El Paso Zoo
Little kid stares at a sea lion from the zoo. 📷 **CARLOS VALDEZ**

THE GREY WOLF *(right)*
The El Paso Zoo
One of the amazing Mexican Wolves at the zoo. 📷 **WILLIAM DUNN**

COLORFUL BIRD *(opposite)*
The El Paso Zoo
This colorful little bird is a longtime resident at the zoo where families
return to say hello to this little friend in the aviary. 📷 **JOYCE WHITESIDE**

SPEED *(previous left)*
Shuffle, deal, let's play! 📷 **BIANCA BOURGEOIS**

HANDS-ON *(previous right)*
Having fun on the monkey bars. 📷 **BIANCA BOURGEOIS**

★ **MORNING PADDLE** *(following left)*
Elephant Butte
Caught a shot of my friends as they took their canoe out for an early
morning paddle on Elephant Butte. 📷 **BRITTANY GIRLE**

FIREWORKS *(following right)*
Wet & Wild, El Paso
Forth of July fireworks. 📷 **RENEE IGLESIAS**

Photographer Directory

Capture El Paso 09 was made possible by local photographers who were willing to share their talents with the rest of us. Here's a list of everyone you'll find in these pages and on the DVD. If you know any of these folks, give them a ring and say thanks for the great book! *(Photographers with Web sites in following list.)*

MEL ADAMS
GILBERT AGUILAR
ANGEL AGUIRRE
MARCELA AGUIRRE
RAYMUNDO AGUIRRE
LAURA ALPERN
ALEJANDRO ALVA
MARTHA ALVAREZ
DIANA AMARO
JESSICA AMBROSE
SAUNDRA ANDERSON
VERONICA ARCHULETA
ISELA AREVALO
J. ENRIQUE ARZAGA
LOUIS AVALOS
CHITO B
IAN BAKER
DIETLINDE BAMBERGER
HELEN BARRY
DORRIS BARRY
ABRAHAM BELMONTES
CASSANDRA BELZER
TRAVIS BERRYMAN
MS. BLANCO
SASHA BLEIFIELD
JULIE BLOOM
JUDITH BONILLA
BERTHA BOURGEOIS
CHERYL BOWMAN
JOAN BRANDL
HELEN BREWER
KYLE BRIGHT
DAVID FRANCISCO BRIONES
DAVID BRIONES
SEAN BRUNA
XOCHITL BUDDÉ
CHARLES BURTON
LORI CALDERON
VICTOR CAMACHO
CRISTINA CAMPOS
CAITLIN CARCERANO
RAFAEL CARRILLO
MIKE CASAS
MICHAEL CASTANEDA
CARLOS CASTANON

CARLOS CASTILLO
ABRIL CASTRO
BERLINDA CAVAZOS
BIANCA CERVANTES
ERNIE CHACON
ERIKA CHAPARRO
JESUS CHAVEZ
GEORGE CHAVEZ
MARIA CIACCIO
IAN CLARK
JUDY COE
BOB COGDELL
JOHN CONCHA
JULIE COOKE
GABRIELA CORDOVA
JADE CORDOVA
ED CORDOVA
SHARON CORDOVA
JORGE CORRAL
STEPHANIE CORREA
GRACE CORTEZ
CHERYL J. COX
AARON CURLEE
MICHEL CYR
MICHAEL DANDO
ASHA DANE'EL
NEIL DAVIS
EDWARD DAY
BENJAMIN DE LEON
OLIVIA DE LEON
KATHY DEBUS
MONIQUE DEITRICK
ANGIE DESANTIAGO
MARIELA DIAZ
GLORIA L. DIAZ
ZYANYA DICKEY
KEVIN DIETER
PETER DINDINGER
DANIEL DOMINGUEZ
HILDA DOMINGUEZ
BARBARA DOUGLAS
ALLA DOVE
WILLIAM DUNN
CARLOS DURAN
VICKIE DYE

HANNAH EBEL
SABRINA ELGUEA
JUANITA ELKINS
FRANK ESCOBAR
IRENE ESCOBAR
FERNIE ESCOBAR
MIKE ESPARZA
RICK ESPINOZA
RUTH ESTRADA
DANIEL ESTRADA ESTRADA
M SYLVIA FABELA
VALERIE FACIO
MICHAEL FARRARO
CECILIA FEMAT
TERESA FERNANDEZ
VANESSA FERNANDEZ
DAISY FERNANDEZ
ESTELLA FERNANDEZ
ERNESTO FERNANDEZ
VALERIA FERNANDEZ
JENNIFER FERRARO
SCOTT FITZPATRICK
RODRIGO FLORES
ROMAN FLORES
LORENZO FLORES, JR.
DAVID FLYNN
JACQUELINE FLYNN
DANIEL FOOTE
GAY FORRISTER
EDGAR FOURNIER
BARBARA FRANKLIN
JANIE FRERICHS
JU-YI FU
JOE GALENSKI
IRMA GALLEGOS
RICK GAMBOA
DAVID GAMEZ
ROBERT GARCIA
FERNIE GARCIA
LAURIE GARCIA
NORMA GARZA
GINA GASTELO
JEN GELAT
MARY ANN GILLISPIE
JOHN GLOVER

LORI GOMEZ
RUBEN GOMEZ
MICHAEL GOMEZ
CHRIS GOMEZ
NORMA GONZALES
ALEX GONZALEZ
ABRIL GONZALEZ
ROBERTO GONZALEZ
BRENDA YANET GONZALEZ
DANIEL GOURLEY
ALYSSA GRANADOS
AIMEE GRANADOS
RICHARD GROAT
CARLOS GUADIAN
ARTURO GUERRA
LILIA GUEVARA
ROBERTA GUIDO
HECTOR GUTIERREZ
CARLOS GUTIERREZ
FABIOLA GUTIERREZ
K HALL
MARVIN HANLEY
AMY HARDY
LESLIE HARRIS
MIRA HATTON
TONIA HEDMAN
JEANNE HENDRICKS
JAMES HENSON
RUDY HERNANDEZ
JAMIE HERNANDEZ
LIIZA HERNANDEZ
SHANNON HIATT
KIMBERLEY HOGGAN
SARAH HOSKINS
DAWN HOWARD
JESSE HUIZAR
ASHLEY HUIZAR
JERRY HUNTER
CARI HUTCHESON
RENEE IGLESIAS
AMBER INGLE
RAY JACKSON
VON HATTEN JAMES
LIZ JARA
MONICA JASSO
JOSEPHINE JIMAREZ-HOWARD
G. WALKER JOHNSON
LONNIE JONES
CHELSEA JORDAN
GINA JUBAR
ELVA PAULINA KABABIE
LAILA KARABASH
MARY KING

SUSAN KISLENGER
GIDEON KOTKOWSKI
EITHAN KOTKOWSKI
AVI KOTKOWSKI
SANDRA KRASSIN
BRIANA LALLY
ANDRES LAMASANGUIANO
VICTORIA LANE
ROBERT LARRAZOLO
ROBETTE LEE
BETH LEFFLER
MARK LENOX
JEANNE LENTZ
RENE LEON
MATTHEW LEON
LAWANNA LINCOLN
JENNIFER LINDNER
GILBERT LOPEZ
VIVIAN LOPEZ
NATHAN LOPEZ
ANA LOPEZ
KATHY LOPEZ
RICHARD LOVE
ELSA LOZADA
JULIANNA LUDLOW DE LEON
ROBBIE LUJAN
MARGARITA LUNA
BILL LYON
CHRISTINA MARENTES
TONI MARIE
TIFFANY MARQUEZ
MARIO MARQUEZ
ESTEBAN MARQUEZ
MIKE MARTINEZ
CARMEN MARTINEZ
TRACY MARTINEZ
LEONARD MARTINEZ
ALBERTO MARTINEZ
ERNESTO D. MARTINEZ
JEFFREY MCCLUER
GINGER MCCLUER
VIRGINIA MCCOY
PATRICK MCKISSACK
LAURA MEDINA
LORI MEDRANO
OMAR MENA
EFRAIN MENDOZA
MARGIE MENDOZA
GINA MENDOZA
BARBARA MENELL
SERGIO MENODZA
MATT METZ
ZITA MEYER

CHRIS MEYER
MARGARET MILLER
CHARLIE MONARREZ
TAMRA MONTES
ANA MONTES
ARLENE MONTOYA
MELODY MOON
SANTIAGO MORALES
MAGGIE MORALES
CAROL MOREAU
TOMMIE MORELOS
ARTHUR MORENO
VALERIE MORGA
MARY ANN MOYA
JASMINE NAHLE
ADRIANA NAJERA-LUDWIG
CRYSTAL NAVARRO
RAY NAVARRO
STEPHANIE NEAL
MARIO NEGRONI

PRISCILLA NEVAREZ
HUMBERTO NEVAREZ
CHAD NORTH
KIM NORTH
STEPHANIE NUNEZ
ALMA NUNEZ
JMAN NUNEZ
DAVID NUNEZ
JOE NUÑEZ
SARITA O'MALLEY
LETICIA OLIVAS
LAURA OLSON
MICHELLE ONTIVEROS
GILBERT ORDONEZ
JOSE OROZCO
SCOT ORSER
AMANDA ORTIZ
EYDIE P
JEANLAURA PADILLA
GABE PADILLA

Capture El Paso 09's most active group:

United Photography
http://unitedphoto.lifepics.com

1,080 Photos
95,595 Votes

ANGEL AGUIRRE
J. ENRIQUE ARZAGA
CHAD BEATY
BRUJO BETANCOURT
SASHA BLEIFIELD
PATRICIA BONILLA
KYLE BRIGHT
GABRIELA CORDOVA
DONNA DAY
EDWARD DAY
CARLOS DURAN
SCOTT FITZPATRICK
TOM GAGE
DAVID GAMEZ

JOSH GARCIA
JOHN GLOVER
RAY JACKSON
JENNIFER LANDRY
VANESSA LIZARRAGA
GILBERT LOPEZ
KATHY LOPEZ
TONI MARIE
JOE NUÑEZ
JMAN NUNEZ
ROBERT PADILLA
MELODY PARRA
CARLOS RAMIREZ
RENE RAMIREZ

MANUEL RAMOS
ROBERT ROQUE
ANGELINE STEWART
TIM SYBRANT
BARBARA SYBRANT
CEASAR TORRES
SOLEDAD VALLEJO
ARIEL VALLEJO
CARLOS VARELA
EDGAR VEGA
MELINDA VEGA
ARMANDO VELA
LEWIS VENECIA
BETH YOST

ROCIO PALACIOS
ELSIE PALMORE
GABE PAPA
QUINN PATTERSON
MARIA PAYAN
ASIEL PAYAN
MIGUEL PDL
CINDY PEPIN
JENNIFER PEREA
ELISA PEREA
DAVID M PEREZ
ANNIE PEREZ
CESAR PEREZ II
JOSEPH PETTY
KYLE PHILLIPS
KYLE PHILLIPS
MAGDALENA PINON
FRANK PIZANA

FRANCESCA PRAT
ELAINE PRENSKY
GARRY PRICE
MICHAEL QUINN
ALBERTO QUIROZ
ONZRA RAMIREZ
RENE RAMIREZ
CYNTHIA RAMIREZ
MIKE RAMIREZ
MATTHEW RAMIREZ
JESSICA RAMIREZ
MANUEL RAMOS
ART RAYON
PATRICIA (TRISH) REDMAN
ALEX REYES
CHRYSALIS REYNA
JAY RIOS
MARIO RIOS

VIVIAN RIVAS
JOYCE RIVERA
ALONZO RIVERA
ROBERT RIVERA
HECTOR RIVEROLL JR
H VALDEZ RO. BERENICE
SOPHIA ROBELE
TROY ROBERTS
LALO RODELA
SERGIO RODRIGUEZ
JOSEPH RODRIGUEZ
VANESSA ROHS
JIM ROLPH
ROBERT ROQUE
LESLIE ROSENTHAL
MATTHEW ROTHBLATT
LISA RULEY
LYNDA RUSHING

SAM RUYBE
BRIANNE SAAD
PATSY SAENZ
STEVE SALAZAR
LUIE SALDANHA
JONATHAN SALDIVAR
VANESSA SANCHEZ
BRIANA SANCHEZ
EDWARD R. SANTA CRUZ
SUSAN SANTA CRUZ
RICHARD SAPIEN
MARGARET SCHAFER
NANCY SCHAUGHENCY
JEAN SCHLITZKUS
GRETCHEN SCHWARZBACH
KEN SEEBURG
MOISES SEGOVIA
MOISES SEGOVIA

ROSEMARY SHIELDS
LORENA SIFUENTES
LYNN SILVERMAN
APRIL SIMANK
ALEX SIMENTAL
J. ANN SJOSTROM
MARY SLAWSON
G. LEWIS SMITH
GABRIELA SORIA
BLANCA SORIA
ANA SORIA
JOWAUNA STEGALL
RON STEWART
HARRY STONE
SYLVIA STROHACKER
TIM SYBRANT
MARIO F. TALAMANTES
MARTHA TORRES

JOSE LUIS TORRES
FEDERICO TORRES
MINNIE TRAVIS
CHRISINDA TREADWELL
CAMILA TRESPALACIOS
MARTHA PAOLA TRESPALACIOS
JESUS VALENZUELA
SOLEDAD VALLEJO
ARIEL VALLEJO
CARLOS VARELA
BRIANA VARGAS
GUILLERMO VAZQUEZ
MELINDA VEGA
EDGAR VEGA
ALLISON VEGA
ARMANDO VELA
PATRICIA VELASCO
DIANE VERA

SAMUEL VILLA
SERGIO VILLA
ALBERT VILLA
DAVID VILLALBA
MISS WATERTIGER
DEBRA WATKINS
JACK WEAVER
JOYCE WHITESIDE
ERIC WILLIAMS
ROBERTH WINTER
ALFREDO ZAMORA
ZACHARY ZEH
JACQUELINE ZUNIGA

If you like what you see in the book and on the companion DVD, be sure to check out these photographers' Web sites. A few even sell prints so you may be able to snag your favorite photos from the project to hang on your wall.

DEANNA AQUIAR
ysletadelsurpueblo.org

JACQUELINE ARROYO
myspace.com/warwingsphotography

NASTASSIA ARTALEJO
facebook.com/nastassiaa

CLARISSA AVALOS
flickr.com/clarebear4

SANDRA BALBOA
flickr.com/photos/lamadrilenya/

CARYL BARQUIN
candccreativephotography.com

CHAD BEATY
vimeo.com/chadbeaty

CHUY BENITEZ
chuybenitez.com

BRUJO BETANCOURT
brujophotography.com

PATRICIA BONILLA
pricelessmemories.lifepics.com

BIANCA BOURGEOIS
flickr.com/blbourgeois12

D BOWDEN
facesplacesandthings.com

AL BRADEN
albradenphoto.com

VANESSA BRADY
gerberadesigns.com

ROBERT BROWN
google.com/profiles/RobertBrownCHB

CLAUDIA CARDENAS
myspace.com/heart_carver

JUSTIN CARMONA
project4studios.deviantart.com/

RICKY CARRASCO
jpgmag.com/people/ximenace

RICARDO CARRILLO
flickr.com/photos/rcarrillo012

MARCOS CASIANO
photo.net/photos/marcos

SAM CASSIANO
sunny999fm.com

FERNIE CENICEROS
myspace.com/fcenicerosphotography

RAY CHIARELLO
jpgmag.com/people/rayjay

BILL CHIZEK
trombone-usa.com/chizek_bill.htm

BRENT CLARKE
highnoonphoto.smugmug.com

JOHN COLLINS
videocompservices.com

SHARO DICKERSON
kulaiphotography.com

LIRA DION
flickr.com/photos/lira-dion/

JEAN-CLAUDE DROUIN
shutterpoint.com/Photos-User.cfm?id=CLAUDE

APRIL EL PASO PORTRAITS
elpasoportraits.com

RAMON ESPARZA
flickr.com/photos/vision18/

ADRIAN ESTORGA
flickr.com/photos/laughmonkey/

AYER ETERNAL
ayereternal.com

JOHN EWART
pbase.com/ewartphotography

CHRIS FENISON
chrisfenison.com

MARVA FONSECA
marva78.deviantart.com/

TOM GAGE
tomgage.com

RUTH GARCIA
sendoutcards.com/22171

GABRIEL GARCIA
flickr.com/photos/gabrielghost

JOSH GARCIA
flickr.com/photos/joshgarciaphotos/

GERARDO GARIBAY
ggaribay.com

BUBBA GELABERT
picasaweb.google.com/bubba.gelabert/

KHUSHROO GHADIALI
flickr.com/photos/khushroo/

BRITTANY GIRLE
flickr.com/photos/britts/

JC GONZALEZ
brightpinktears.com

MELISSA GONZALEZ
facebook.com/profile.php?id=1377928601&ref=profile

WALTER HERRIT
SensualGlamourPhotos.com

SCOTT HINCHMAN
srhdesigns.com

ERIKA JACKSON
flickr.com/photos/16884461@N00/

STEVE JOLLY
jollyshouse.com

MAURICIO LARA
myspace.com/mlphotography123

JEANETTE LEYVA
myspace.com/milsaggy_jenny

JOSE LIMON
onemodelplace.com/member.cfm?P_ID=32469

LUIS LUCIO
myspace.com/arkoiris_de_mariguana

JOSH LUTTRELL
jgluttrell.smugmug.com/

ISAAC MEDINA
facebook.com/home.php?#/pages/iSax-Photography/121277185165?ref=ts

YVIANA MENDOZA
myspace.com/an_affair_forever

MONICA MOLINAR
myspace.com/itsnotalovesong5

JERZY MOLON
jerzyphotography.axspace.com

CRYSTAL MORTON
facebook.com/ILoveMyHarley

LAURA NATIVIDAD
flickr.com/photos/yayita

CHUY NAVA
southwestdrags.com

JEANETTE NEVAREZ A.
myspace.com/cool_pettuney

TIM O'MALLEY
omalleycat.us

JOSE OLIVAS
mardyn.me

ADRIANA ONATE
flickr.com/photos/adrianaelisa/

ROBERT PADILLA
robertpadilla.net

GEORGE PADILLA
padillaphoto.com

MELODY PARRA
melparphoto.com

LETICIA PENA
myspace.com/refractiveelementsphoto

PRISCILLA PORTILLO
delpueblopress.biz

DENNIS QUINTANA
flickr.com/photos/taosjedi/

CARLOS RAMIREZ
sandraspics.com

ANDY RAMIREZ
SAIKOSISFILMS.com

ALICIA RASCON
mylatinitas.com

ELIAS REVELES
jpgmag.com/people/hurst1

ANNETT RITTER
kokophoto.de

FERMIN ROBLEDO
flickr.com/photos/25520089@N03/

ISABEL RODRIGUEZ
myspace.com/adrianarich

RUBEN ROMERO
viewmorepics.myspace.com/index.cfm?fuseaction=user.viewPicture&friendID=18432304&albumId=2716857

MIRANDA ROSS
mirandarossphotography.ifp3.com

RIANNON ROWLEY
facebook.com/riannon32

DONALD SCHARF
bond-photo.com

MARK SCHRIER
marksclickart.imagekind.com

JIM SCHWARZBACH
Jim.AM

DIANE SIERRA
deluxephotovideo.com/

DIETER STEINBECK
edepfau.de

ANGELINE STEWART
flickr.com/nurselovegash

KERRIGAN SWAN-GARCIA
chatnoirphotographie.com

GEORGE TAUSIANI
gvphoto.net

CEASAR TORRES
jpgmag.com/people/imagineerthat

IGNACIO TORRES
starkaesthetic.blogspot.com/

ADAM ULLOA
myspace.com/lovelyshoes

CARLOS VALDEZ
flickr.com/photos/28953625@N07/

NEREIDA VALLES
standtallandgrow.blogspot.com/

NICOLE VARELA
flickr.com/photos/nikki_v/

LEWIS VENECIA
jpgmag.com/people/manfrotto

ENRIQUE VILLAR
therainmakerphotography.web.officelive.com

JACQUELINE VILLEGAS
myspace.com/sprettybunny

PATRICK-DAVID WALKER
thedarkermist.storm-artists.net/

LISA WILLIAMS
myspace.com/picturedlw

BETH YOST
community.webshots.com/user/bethlynn0614?vhost=community

Chapter Introduction Photographers

The many photographers listed below helped shape the introduction page of each chapter. Many thanks to these fine folks (listed in order of appearance from left to right, top to bottom):

Friendly Faces: Gerardo Garibay, Patricia Bonilla, Brent Clarke, Julianna Ludlow De Leon, Jay Rios, Jeffrey McCluer, Avi Kotkowski, Allison Vega, Mauricio Lara, Miss Watertiger, Chad Beaty, Lori Calderon, Brent Clarke, Ricky Carrasco, Ricky Carrasco, Crystal Morton, Patricia Bonilla, Sandra Balboa, Elsa Lozada, Fermin Robledo, Brent Clarke, Gerardo Garibay, Martha Paola Trespalacios, Ricardo Carrillo, Allison Vega, Carlos Varela, Marva Fonseca, George Padilla, Richard Groat, Elva Paulina Kababie, Miss Watertiger, Alonzo Rivera

Arts, Food & Culture: J. Ann Sjostrom, Bubba Gelabert, Neil Davis, Minnie Travis, Ricky Carrasco, Bianca Bourgeois, Brent Clarke, April El Paso Portraits, Minnie Travis, Cesar Perez Ii, Elias Reveles, Melody Parra, David Briones, Ricky Carrasco, Vanessa Brady, Chito B, Fermin Robledo, Erika Jackson, Fernie Ceniceros, Miss Watertiger, Ayer Eternal, Omar Mena, Erika Jackson, Ricky Carrasco, Carlos Ramirez, Cesar Perez Ii, Roberto Gonzalez, Sharo Dickerson, Hector Riveroll Jr

Pets: Beth Yost, Diana Amaro, Von Hatten James, Erika Jackson, Dennis Quintana, Martha Paola Trespalacios, Carlos Valdez, Ruth Estrada, Angel Aguirre, Elias Reveles, George Tausiani, Luie Saldanha, Carlos Varela, April El Paso Portraits, Miss Watertiger, Martha Paola Trespalacios, Miss Watertiger, Laura Natividad, Beth Yost, Jean-Claude Drouin, Carol Moreau, Riannon Rowley, Helen Brewer, Martha Paola Trespalacios, Brent Clarke, Valerie Facio, Sandra Balboa, Beth Yost, Helen Brewer, Ray Navarro, Miss Watertiger, Cindy Pepin, Michel Cyr

Scapes of All Sorts: Kim North, Ana Soria, Julianna Ludlow De Leon, George Padilla, Vickie Dye, Gilbert Lopez, Miss Watertiger, Avi Kotkowski, John Ewart, Sandra Balboa, Miss Watertiger, Minnie Travis, Bubba Gelabert, Rene Leon, Blanca Soria, Ricky Carrasco, Mike Martinez, Steve Jolly, Gerardo Garibay, Miss Watertiger, Olivia De Leon, Sharo Dickerson, Avi Kotkowski, Ray Chiarello, Shannon Hiatt, John Glover, Jeffrey McCluer, Valerie Facio, Mark Schrier, Kim North

Newsworthy: George Tausiani, Elias Reveles, Ricky Carrasco, George Tausiani, George Tausiani, Erika Jackson, Ray Navarro, Crystal Morton, John Concha, Chad Beaty, Mike Ramirez, Beth Yost, Quinn Patterson, Neil Davis, Ricky Carrasco, Kim North, Chad Beaty, Eydie P, George Tausiani, Bertha Bourgeois, David Briones, Miss Watertiger, Ceasar Torres, Miss Watertiger, Bianca Bourgeois, John Concha, Lewis Venecia, Dawn Howard, Jim Schwarzbach, Bertha Bourgeois, Ricky Carrasco

Schools & Institutions: John Glover, Al Braden, Erika Jackson, Kerrigan Swan-Garcia, Elias Reveles, Sabrina Elguea, Lori Medrano, Elias Reveles, G. Lewis Smith, William Dunn, Ricky Carrasco, Kerrigan Swan-Garcia, Lewis Venecia, Patrick-David Walker, Elias Reveles, Angeline Stewart, Enrique Villar, April El Paso Portraits, Gilbert Lopez, Jacqueline Villegas, Mario Rios, Mark Lenox, Ricky Carrasco, Lorenzo Flores, Ruth Estrada, Ruth Estrada, Efrain Mendoza, Jacqueline Zuniga, Frank Escobar, Lisa Williams, Chad Beaty

Everyday Life: Erika Jackson, Julianna Ludlow De Leon, Erika Jackson, Michelle Ontiveros, Sharo Dickerson, Elias Reveles, Jerzy Molon, John Ewart, Daniel Estrada Estrada, George Tausiani, Matt Metz, Minnie Travis, David Briones, Sarita O'Malley, Miss Watertiger, Miss Watertiger, Scot Orser, Patricia Bonilla, Ricky Carrasco, Ricky Carrasco, Robert Garcia, Sharo Dickerson, Bubba Gelabert, George Tausiani, Josh Garcia, J. Ann Sjostrom, Ricky Carrasco, Avi Kotkowski, Miss Watertiger, Lori Calderon, Patrick-David Walker, Gerardo Garibay

Sports & Recreation: Ceasar Torres, Judy Coe, Jeffrey McCluer, Avi Kotkowski, Fernie Ceniceros, Ray Navarro, Lewis Venecia, Andres Lamasanguiano, Jeffrey McCluer, Riannon Rowley, Lalo Rodela, Albert Villa, Mira Hatton, Eithan Kotkowski, David Gamez, Lewis Venecia, Khushroo Ghadiali, Chrisinda Treadwell, Ray Navarro, Brent Clarke, Avi Kotkowski, Angel Aguirre, George Padilla, Ariel Vallejo, Fermin Robledo, Martha Paola Trespalacios, Eithan Kotkowski, Hannah Ebel, Robert Garcia, Jeffrey McCluer, Ray Navarro

Prize Winners

When picking from more than 9,000 photos, it's difficult to nail down what separates the best from the rest — especially when so many photos are so good. To help, we enlisted thousands of local folks to vote for their favorite shots. The response was epic: 727,919 votes were cast. The voting helped shape what would eventually be published in this book. Along the way, the votes produced the prize winners below. Here's a brief explanation of how prizes were determined:

People's Choice: This one's as simple as it sounds. The photo that gets the highest score, according to how folks voted, is given this award. We picked a different winner for the Editors' Choice award, but we think local folks are pretty smart too, so we wanted to reward the photo that people like the most. This is also one of the ways we figure out the grand prize.

Editors' Choice: This award goes to the photo our editors determine to be the best in a chapter. Sometimes it'll be a photo that fits the chapter so well that it stands out above the rest. Other times it could be a photo that is technically excellent. Our editors poured over submitted photos daily during the contest and were constantly thinking about which photo should be the "Editors' Choice." Our editors also helped pick the grand prize photo from a pool of People's Choice photos.

People's Choice in Friendly Faces
PHOTO BY FERNIE CENICEROS
page 14

People's Choice in Arts, Culture & Food
PHOTO BY RICKY CARRASCO
page 20

People's Choice in Pets
PHOTO BY MARTHA PAOLA TRESPALACIOS
page 40

People's Choice in Scapes of All Sorts
PHOTO BY GEORGE PADILLA
page 78

People's Choice in Newsworthy
PHOTO BY CARLOS VALDEZ
page 92

People's Choice in Schools & Institutions
PHOTO BY SHARO DICKERSON
page 107

People's Choice in Everyday Life
PHOTO BY LIRA DION
page 119

People's Choice in Sports & Recreation
PHOTO BY JERZY MOLON
page 125

Editors' Choice in Friendly Faces
PHOTO BY MARVA FONSECA
page 10

Editors' Choice in Arts, Culture & Food
PHOTO BY CESAR PEREZ II
page 36

Editors' Choice in Pets
PHOTO BY NASTASSIA ARTALEJO
page 46

Editors' Choice in Scapes of All Sorts
PHOTO BY AVI KOTKOWSKI
page 76

Editors' Choice in Newsworthy
PHOTO BY GEORGE TAUSIANI
page 94

Editors' Choice in Schools & Institutions
PHOTO BY MARVIN HANLEY
page 108

Editors' Choice in Everyday Life
PHOTO BY GERARDO GARIBAY
page 115

Editors' Choice in Sports & Recreation
PHOTO BY BRITTANY GIRLE
page 138

Grand Prize Winner
PHOTO BY BRENT CLARKE
page 131

Cover Shot Winner
PHOTO BY RAY NAVARRO
cover, page 79

Thank you!